Sports

Dance

by Nick Rebman

FOCUS READERS

www.focusreaders.com

Focus Readers is distributed by North Star Editions:
sales@northstareditions.com | 888-417-0195

Produced for Focus Readers by Red Line Editorial.

Photographs ©: Creatista/Shutterstock Images, cover, 1; Iakov Filimonov/Shutterstock Images, 4; Satyrenko/Shutterstock Images, 7, 16 (bottom left), 16 (bottom right); Photobac/Shutterstock Images, 9, 16 (top right); SpeedKingz/Shutterstock Images, 11; Photobac/Shutterstock Images, 13, 16 (top left); kali9/iStockphoto, 15

ISBN
978-1-63517-917-0 (hardcover)
978-1-64185-019-3 (paperback)
978-1-64185-221-0 (ebook pdf)
978-1-64185-120-6 (hosted ebook)

Library of Congress Control Number: 2018931983

Printed in the United States of America
Mankato, MN
May, 2018

About the Author

Nick Rebman enjoys reading, drawing, and traveling to places where he doesn't speak the language. He lives in Minnesota.

Table of Contents

Dance

Dance is fun.

Dancers move their arms.

Dancers move their legs.

Some dancers wear **tights**.

Some dancers wear **skirts**.

Some dancers wear shoes.

skirt

tights

shoes

Safety

Dancers **stretch**.

They stretch before

they dance.

This keeps dancers safe.

How to Move

This dancer taps her feet.

The taps make noise.

It is called tap dance.

This dancer holds a bar.

He bends his **knees**.

He turns his feet.

bar

knee

There are many kinds

of dance.

They are all fun to learn.

Glossary

knees

stretch

skirts

tights

Index